Get Free, Stay Free

A Teaching Manual for:

Personal Healing, Deliverance

and

Personal Spiritual Warfare

John 8:32 Ye shall know the truth, and
The truth shall make you free

by
Thomas and Fay Velez
His Spirit In Us Ministries

Table of Contents

Introduction

This book is used as a teaching manual/workbook for a class of this same name:

Get Free, Stay Free
Personal Healing, Deliverance,
and Personal Spiritual Warfare

The Personal Spiritual Warfare material is extensive, and as such, is contained in a separate book of the same name, written by Thomas Velez.

This book is intended to show you how, and lead you through, the process of understanding and getting free of the demonic strongholds in your life, as well as from the emotional and spiritual strongholds and past trauma in your life. Many times, our problems are inherited from our ancestor's problems, actions, words and behavior. Many times, we grow up believing that these things are just normal life. Examples of that would include how we treat our spouses, children, and others. It can include problems like poverty, mindsets and attitudes, alcohol, etc. It also can include many of our responses to other people's actions or words or to our circumstances or unfortunate surprises, e.g.: anger, frustration, depression, rejection, pessimism. Sometimes, our current problems are related to past trauma in our lives, or even to our own bad choices and behaviors.

This class will also teach you much about how to heal various medical problems and refer you to a few great healing ministry books by proven, well recognized Christian healing ministers. This class, will introduce you to some of their concepts, which we routinely demonstrate real, actual, visually confirmed, instantaneous healing miracles, and teach you to do them also.

This book is intended to be a reference manual and a training workbook, that you can use to get free of many of these problems and learn how to stay free.

THIS BOOK IS NOT MEANT TO BE A REPLACEMENT FOR THE CHRISTIAN BIBLE OR DOCTRINE, BUT A PRACTICAL APPLICATION OF THEM FOR YOUR OWN LIFE, AND THOSE AROUND YOU.

May God open the eyes of your understanding and bless you.

To our Lord and only Savior, Jesus Christ, be all glory, and honor, power, and dominion.

About the Authors:

Thomas and Fay Velez are ordained Christian International (CI) ministers. They lead the Prophetic Healing and Deliverance Ministry at the CI Headquarters Vision Church in Santa Rosa Beach, Florida and lead the daily prayer meetings there also. They are also on the Prophetic Teams there and have a traveling ministry.

Thomas holds a master's degree from CI in Biblical Studies, and functions in the fivefold office of a Prophet and Teacher. He has been teaching on the gifts of the Holy Spirit, including the Prophetic, the Book of Revelation and personal spiritual warfare for over 40 years, with the guidance of the Holy Spirit helping him to understand many of the complexities of the Bible, especially future prophetic events. Thomas is also a retired Aerospace Engineer with 50 years' experience.

Fay Velez also holds a Biblical degree from CI, and functions in the fivefold office of a Prophet. She is especially gifted in the discerning of spirits, deliverance, prophetic counseling, spiritual warfare, and intercession.

Thomas and Fay have been teaching and ministering together on the gifts of the Holy Spirit, prophesying over individuals, doing personal deliverances and administering the Lord's healing through the glorious name of Jesus Christ, for over 30 years as a team ministry.

They have personally led many to a saving knowledge of Jesus Christ as their Savior, and to the Baptism of the Holy Spirit with the evidence of speaking in tongues.

Chapter 1: Freedom, Unforgiveness, Rejection

Freedom:

What is freedom, how you lose it, and how you keep it.

Romans 6:14: For sin will no longer be a master over you, since you are not under Law [as slaves], but under [unmerited] grace [as recipients of God's favor and mercy].

Freedom is defined in the dictionary as, the state of not being imprisoned or enslaved, and being able to speak or act without hinderance or restraint.

Inside or Spiritual freedom is having the ability to obey God and choose His will for our lives. This freedom allows us to be free socially and spiritually and allows us to prosper both materially and spiritually.

How demons enter:
They enter by open doors. Demons are spirit beings, and they temp, deceive, accuse, condemn, steal, afflict, kill and destroy.

John 10:10: The thief comes only to steal and kill and destroy; I have come that they may have life and have it to the full.

There are many spirits that keep us from being free.

Unforgiveness:

Matthew *6:14-15 For if you forgive others their trespasses your heavenly Father will also forgive you. But if you do not forgive others then your Father will not forgive your trespasses.*

Unforgiveness gives the devil legal ground in our life. It puts us into the enemy's hands.

It stands between us and God. It stops our spiritual growth.

It stops our physical healing and our deliverance.

Unforgiveness causes anger, bitterness, revenge, hatred, malice, and resentment.

Unforgiveness steals your joy, your happiness and your peace.

Unforgiveness prayer:

Heavenly Father, You are Holy and righteous, You are perfect in justice. Lord, I stand before You and I confess that I have not forgiven others as You have commanded me to. Lord, right now, I forgive everyone that has hurt me, and I release them to You Lord. Lord, I ask You to forgive me, and cleanse me from my sin. God forgive me for any way I have partnered in an ungodly way with unforgiveness, bitterness, anger, or resentment. Lord, help me to thoroughly place these people and the wrong they have caused me into your hands in Jesus name. Lord, I pray that your will will be done in my life, and in the lives of people that have hurt me. Lord, I invite You into any painful memories, I have concerning what was done to me, in Jesus name. Lord, heal any wounds I have received. Thank you, Lord for all this in the name of Jesus. Amen

Rejection:

Rejection is defined in the Webster's dictionary as to refuse a person recognition, acceptance, to cast away as worthless, or to discard.

Rejection makes you feel not wanted, and makes you have self-pity and makes you give up.

Rejection is one of Satan's most effective tools he uses against a believer, and it is a stronghold in many people's life.

Rejection causes people to have low self-esteem, to feel like they are ugly, having anger, being rebellious.

The root cause of rejection has to be destroyed, pulled up and cut off and then the spirit cast out.

Rejection Prayer:

In the name of Jesus, I renounce any inherited spirits of rejection that have been passed down to me by my ancestors. I forgive my ancestors for passing those spirits down to me, and I renounce them, and reject them from my life in the name of Jesus. I renounce every spirit of rejection, the spirits of fear of rejection, self-rejection, and perceived rejection that may have entered my life when I was conceived or born or that entered at any other time, in the name of Jesus. I close every door against spirits of rejection and cancel every legal right that rejection has had to operate in my life. I command the spirits of inherited rejection, fear of rejection, self-rejection and perceived rejection to loose their hold on me now, in the name of Jesus. Amen

Chapter 2: Fear, Abuse

Fear:

Natural fear is a natural reaction to a danger in our surroundings,

Spirit of Fear is a tormenting fear, and it is not from God, and it is not a natural fear.

The spirit of fear opens the door to other demonic spirits, and its goal is to cause us to live in torment.

It is a paralyzing fear that controls us.

Some ways the spirit of Fear manifest can be: worry, insecurity, nervousness, abandonment or anxiety.

The spirit of fear opens the door for the spirit of infirmity.

The Spirit of fear steals our identity, our anointing, our vision, and our confidence.

Fear Prayer:

Lord, I love You and I come before You today, and in the name of Jesus I command any spirit of fear that has me paralyzed and bound to go now from me and go to where Jesus sends you, in Jesus name. I command all doubt and unbelief to go, in Jesus name. Lord, I ask You to put your loving arms around me and Lord let me feel your love and your touch in a special way, in Jesus name. Lord, I thank You that I am free from fear and the forces that has had me bound. Lord I thank You that who the Son sets free is free indeed and that I am free today in Jesus name. Lord, I ask You to fill every empty place in me with your Holy Spirit where any spirt of fear was at and I thank You Lord that I will walk in the knowing that greater is He who lives in me than, he who lives in the world. Lord, thank You that no weapon formed against me will prosper, and that I am a victor not a victim in Jesus name, and that the fear is gone in Jesus name. Amen

Abuse:

Abuse can be defined in Webster dictionary as, to inflict physical or emotional mistreatment or injury on someone purposely, or to engage in sexual activity with a child, or to attack harshly with words.

Abuse causes one to have fear, guilt, shame, anxiety, depression and feel intimidated.

Abuse destroys our self-worth.

Abuse is not just physical it can be emotional abuse as well.

Emotional abuse is when someone chips away at your feelings of self-worth and your independence, leaving you feeling that there is no way out, or without your abusive partner you will have nothing. They try to make you feel powerless.

God does not condone any kind of abuse:

1Cor. 13:4-7 Love is patient, love is kind. It does not envy, it does not boast, it is not proud. It does not dishonor others, it is not self-seeking, it is not easily angered, it keeps no record of wrongs. Loves does not delight in evil but rejoice with the truth. It always protects, always trusts, always hopes always perseveres.

Jesus came to the world for abused victims:

Isaiah 61:1 The Spirit of the Lord God is upon me, because the Lord has anointed and commissioned me, to bring good news to the humble and afflicted;

He has sent me to bind up the brokenhearted, to proclaim release to the captives and freedom to prisoners.

Abuse Prayer:

Lord, I lift myself up to You today and I ask You to heal and touch every place in my life that has been hurt or damaged, in Jesus name. Lord, heal all pain and wounds, in Jesus name. Lord, heal my broken heart, in Jesus name. Lord, set me free from any bitterness, anger, resentment, or unforgiveness, in Jesus name. Lord, heal my emotions and let me know that I am loved by You. Lord, set me free from any guilt or blame that I have allowed to attach itself to me, in Jesus name. Lord, heal my emotional and physical pain I have encountered, in Jesus name. Lord, heal the anguish deep inside of me, in Jesus name. Lord, touch me from the top of my head to the soles of my feet with your soothing balm and your healing love, in Jesus name. I command all negative emotions that are inside of me to go, in Jesus name. Lord, fill me up with your love, your peace and your joy, in Jesus name. Lord, flood me with your presence, in Jesus name. Lord, restore me mentally, physically, emotionally, spiritually and financially, in Jesus name, and let me see myself as You see me and that is as a child of the King, one that is Royalty, one that is an overcomer, and one that is victorious, in Jesus name. Amen

Chapter 3: Generational Curses, Fortune Telling, Halloween

Generational Curses

Generational Curses are defined as the sins that our ancestors have committed, and they are passed down to us from generation to generation.

Deu. 5:9 You shall not bow down to them or worship them; for I, the Lord your God, am a jealous God, punishing the children for the sin of the parents to the third and fourth generation of those who hate me.

Generational Curses must be cut off and cast out. If they are not, the devil has a legal right to continue these curses from generation to generation.

Generational Curse Prayer:

Lord, we come before You to confess the sins of our ancestors that have been committed against You, in Jesus name. We close every door where the enemy has had an open door to enter, whether it was from our ancestors or from us, in Jesus name. Lord, forgive us, in Jesus name. Lord, cleanse us with the blood of Jesus and purify us, in Jesus name. In the name of Jesus, we cut off every curse that has been passed down our family line. Thank you, Lord, for sending your Son to die for our freedom. In the name of Jesus, we cut ourselves off from any vows, contracts, or agreements we have made knowingly or unknowingly with the devil. We renounce these agreements and we decree we are set free, in Jesus name. We thank your Lord, that all curses that have been passed down our blood line are void and null, in Jesus name. We reject all these curses, and we choose to walk in the blessings of Abraham, in Jesus name. We decree that generational curses of sickness, poverty, rage, additions, are cancelled in our life and in our family's life, in Jesus name. Thank you, Lord, that we have been made a new creation in You, and from this day forward we choose to walk in freedom, in Jesus name. We are set free from all chains and bondages, in Jesus name, and we stand strong in our new identity, and we declare we are of a different blood line, and that blood line is the blood line of You Lord, in Jesus name. We tell you devil you have no more powers over us, mentally, physically, financially, or spiritually, in Jesus name, because who the Son sets free is free indeed, and we are free in Jesus name. Amen

Fortune Telling, Psychic, & Mediums

I know these three have different aspects about them, but I am going to just group them together as I talk about them, because they are all three demonic, and they are used pretty much the same way. Some of them just go deeper into the demonic, but the end results are pretty much the same.

Wikipedia defined them as a practice of predicting information about a person's life. Using tools like crystal balls, tarot cards, or seeing into the demonic world or talking to the dead or predicting your future.

These three spirits are nothing to mess with. They are powerful if you open the door to them.

These practices are forbidden by God

Deuteronomy 18:10-13 Let no one be found among you who sacrifice their son or daughter in the fire, who practices divination or sorcery, interprets omens, engages in witchcraft, or casts spells, or who is a medium or spiritist, or who consults the dead. Anyone who does these things is detestable to the Lord; because of these same detestable practices the Lord your God will drive out those nations before you. You must be blameless, before the Lord your God.

These different practices honor the demonic spirits, and God calls them detestable things and He hates it.

Galatians 5:19-21The act of the flesh are obvious: sexual immorality, impurity and debauchery; idolatry and witchcraft, hatred, discord, jealousy, fits of rage, selfish ambition, dissensions, factions and envy, drunkenness, orgies, and the like. I warn you, as I did before, that those who live like this will not inherit the kingdom of God.

Prayer to renounce fortune telling, Psychic or mediums:

Lord, I renounce and cancel every involvement that I have had knowingly or unknowingly with fortune telling, Psychic reading or mediums, in Jesus name. Lord, I ask You to forgive me for having any part in this, in Jesus name. In the name of Jesus, I bind and cut off and cast out every spirit of fortune telling, Psychic reading or mediums, that I have allowed to enter into my life. In Jesus name, I break off every chain and every stronghold off of myself now. I break off every negative word, thought or action directed to me from any form of dealing with these practices, in Jesus name. Lord, I give You praise that I am victorious through You and that You have made me strong and that You are my fortress and You are a strong tower for me to run to, in Jesus name. Lord, raise me up to be able to overcome everything that would try to pull me away from You, in Jesus name. Lord, I put on the whole armor of God, and I thank You that I am able to stand against the devil's schemes, and that no weapon formed against me will prosper, in Jesus name. Lord, as I submit to You, I thank You that the devil will flee, in Jesus name. Thank You, Lord, for being my protector, my rock, my salvation, and my fortress, in Jesus name. Lord, I give You praise for setting me free, and I thank You that who the Son sets free is free indeed, in Jesus name. Amen

Halloween:

The name Halloween comes from the 1500's, and it is the evening before All Hollow's Day or All Saints Day.

The meaning of Halloween comes from an ancient Celtic harvest festival, and it is recognized as the day when the souls of the dead supposedly could mingle with the living. They also believed during this night, witches and evil spirits are free to roam the earth.

But now people look at Halloween as just a fun night. But people are deceived;

Halloween is not based on godly themes such as peace, freedom, salvation.

It brings fear, oppression and bondage.

Philippians 4:8 Finally, believers, whatever is true, whatever is honorable and worthy of respect, whatever is right and confirmed by God's word, whatever is pure and wholesome, whatever is lovely and brings peace, whatever is admirable and of good report; if there is anything excellent, if there is anything worthy of praise, think continually on these things [center your mind on them, and implant them in your heart].

Halloween is an abomination practice and God hates it.

Halloween honors evil spirits and the dead spirits.

There are all kinds of animal and children sacrifices on Halloween night.

The Bible plainly denounces this:

Lev. 20:6 says: I will set my face against anyone who turns to mediums and spirits to prostitute themselves by following them. And I will cut them off from their people.

1Samuel 15:23 says: "For rebellion is as [serious as] the sin of divination (fortune-telling), and disobedience is as [serious as] false religion and idolatry. Because you have rejected the word of the Lord, He also has rejected you as king.

Halloween Prayer:

In Jesus name, I renounce any involvements I have had participating in Halloween knowingly or unknowingly and Lord, I ask You to forgive me in Jesus name.

In Jesus name, I bind every evil force that has tried to operate against me and my family. I cancel the spirit of witchcraft that has tried to operate over me, and I silence your operation, in Jesus name. Lord, I decree that, that curse will no longer affect me any longer, in Jesus name.

Lord, I ask You to fill every empty place in me with your Holy Spirit and cleanse me, purify me, in Jesus name. Lord, I ask You to send your fire to apprehend the enemies that have tried to come against me, in Jesus name. Lord, let your fire burn up every negative contract against my life. Lord, set me free from all practices of Halloween in Jesus name. Lord, let me feel your love, let me encounter you, and your presence, in Jesus name. Lord, protect me and keep me safe, in Jesus name. I say no weapon formed against me will prosper, and that no evil will befall me, in Jesus name. Thank You Lord, that I dwell in the secret places of the Most High.

Chapter 4: Negative Soul Ties, Spirit Transfer, Out-of-Body

Soul Ties

Soul ties are the spiritual union of and between people

- *Mark 10:7-8 For this reason a man shall leave his father and mother and be **joined** to his wife, and the two shall become one flesh'; so then **they are no longer two**, but one flesh.*

- *1 Cor 6:15-17 Do you not know that your bodies are members of Christ? Shall I then take the members of Christ and **make them members** of a harlot? Certainly not! Or do you not know that he who is **joined** to a harlot is one body with her? For "the two," He says, "shall become one flesh." But he who is joined to the Lord is one spirit with Him.*

After the sex, they are still members of each other!

Godly union/soul tie with spouse is good.

Ungodly union/soul tie is obviously bad.

Union/soul tie is like an umbilical cord between people.

Concept of connecting their spirits

Godly soul/spirit tie Remember: *1 Cor 17 But he who is joined to the Lord is one spirit with Him*

The soul tie/umbilical cord between people allow spirit transfers between them, even without the people realizing it.

There are no barriers/safeguards to stop the transfers

    Like being behind the firewall in a computer network server

Godly Soul Ties:

Godly union/soul tie with spouse is good.

1 Cor 7: 12 But to the rest speak I, not the Lord: If any brother hath a wife that believeth not, and she be pleased to dwell with him, let him not put her away.

13 And the woman which hath an husband that believeth not, and if he be pleased to dwell with her, let her not leave him.

14 For the unbelieving husband is sanctified by the wife, and the unbelieving wife is sanctified by the husband: else were your children unclean; but now are they holy.

That Godly union/soul tie from the good spouse can be sanctification for the ungodly spouse.

Our God is a God of family salvation. Part of that is by Godly-soul ties.

Ungodly Soul Ties/Umbilical Cords

Ungodly soul ties can be formed by sex outside of marriage.

Soul ties can also be formed by pledges, vows, etc.

Blood covenants (blood brothers, dedications, etc.)

Fraternities, sororities, secret lodges, etc.

Demons, addictions, manipulative control, dependency, strong attractions, lusts, fear, afflictions, confusion, depression, torment, etc. can transfer at will through the connecting umbilical cord-because there are no barriers.

Can be reason for unexplained/irrational behavior.

- Staying in abusive relationship
- Failure to perceive conditions correctly
- Unexpected or continuing temptations or torments
- Concern someone else is knowing or controlling you

Soul ties must be cut after a divorce!

1. Renounced, and

2. Cut, with the name and blood of Jesus

Also, occult uses umbilical cord (aka silver/gray cord) to stay connected to their soul in their body when they do out-of-body spirit travel

> If you suspect such intrusion, command the umbilical cord (silver cord/gray cord) to be severed and their spirit to become disoriented and lost and leave your area

Do not tolerate the demonic:

Come against them with the name and blood of Jesus

Repentance Prayer is necessary.

In the name of Jesus Christ, I hereby reject and renounce any involvement in pre-marital or extra-marital sex. I hereby reject and renounce any involvement with any other ungodly soul-tie connections, including but not limited to any ungodly vows, blood covenants, dedications, memberships, secret societies, rituals, or agreements. Right now, in the name and power authority and blood of Jesus Christ, I reject and cut off any and all soul-ties formed by or from any of these things. In the name, power, authority and blood of Jesus Christ, I also reject and cut off any soul ties from any ex-spouses. In Jesus name, I command any of those fragmented pieces of soul ties to go back to wherever they came from, and I command any godly soul tie pieces that originated in me, to come back to me.

Chapter 5: Pride, Chaos, Occult, Masons, & Spirit Religions

Pride & Chaos:

People have a spirit, not just a physical body

　　part of them attached to the spirit realm

Christians marked by Holy Spirit. Entire spirit world sees it

Christians can be attacked from the spirit realm

Evil spirits can work through people against you

1 Peter 5:8 [Be sober], [be vigilant]; because your adversary the devil, as a roaring lion, walketh about, seeking whom he may devour:

Behavior and attitude affect your vulnerability

Devil is looking for your vulnerability

*James 3:16 For **where envy and self-seeking exist, confusion and every evil thing are there**.*

Envy and self-seeking open the gates to every evil thing

Must wait on God: PATIENCE

*James 4:6-7 "God **resists the proud** But gives grace to the humble". Therefore **submit to God.** Resist the devil and he will flee from you*

If you are proud or will not submit to God, the devil will constantly bother you

Pride and self-seeking is major reason for strife and chaos

Repentance Prayer is necessary.

Father God, in Jesus name I ask You to recognize any pride in my life, and forgive me for my pride, selfishness, and my own self-seeking. I repent of this and will do my best to submit to you, and to be more Christ-like and to follow You in obedience and humility, representing You and Jesus as best I can.

In the name of Jesus Christ, we bind every demonic spirit in my life involving pride, selfishness, and my own self-seeking. In Jesus name, we take authority over these spirits and command them to come out and leave us and our families now, and never return, and no replacements to come back in their stead. In Jesus name.

Occult:

My definition: people working with demonic beings

Various definitions: dealing with or in hidden, secret, or mysterious things

> Witchcraft, including

> Wicca: Officially recognized religion in USA

> Involves secret rituals/potions to get demons to do something: e.g.: conjuring; attacking; control of the mind/will/love/emotions of someone

People enticed by:

1. Power, or

2. Curiosity, or

3. Wanting to know the future

Other Occult practices:

Fortune telling (divination), Astrology & Horoscopes

> You are choosing to allow demonic to influence/manipulate/control your future

De 18:10-12 (NKJV) There shall not be found among you anyone who makes his son or daughter pass through the fire, or who uses divination, or is a soothsayer, or an augur, or a sorcerer,
*11 Or a charmer, or a medium, or a wizard, or a necromancer. 12 **For all who do these things are an abomination to the Lord**,*

Tarot Cards: seeking hidden knowledge, future, etc.

Séances: seeking the dead departed spirits

Channeling/familiar spirits/spirit guides/assigned animal spirit guides: communicating with demons

Ouija Board: communicating with demons

Magic: Real magic is demonic displays/tricks in our physical realm to impress, lure, or make fearful.

There is no good (real) magic: White magic still involves demons

Det 18:10-12 (Message Bible) Don't you dare sacrifice your son or daughter in the fire. Don't practice divination, sorcery, fortunetelling, witchery, 11 casting spells, holding séances, or channeling with the dead. 12 People who do these things are an abomination to GOD.

Satanism: obviously demonic

Repentance Prayer is necessary.

Father God, in Jesus name I ask You to forgive me for any involvement in: witchcraft, fortune telling, astrology, horoscopes, Ouija Boards, Tarot cards, sorcery, seances, casting spells, channeling, Satanism and satanic rituals, and any relationships with or consulting with spirit guides, or communication with devils or departed human beings, conjuring, and involvement in the occult in any form. I repent of this and will do my best to submit to you, and to be more Christ-like and to follow You in obedience and humility, and to represent You and Jesus as best I can.

In the name of Jesus Christ, we bind every demonic spirit in my life involving any of these things. In Jesus name, we take authority over these spirits and command them to come out and leave us and our families now, and never return, and no replacements to come back in their stead. In Jesus name.

Other Spirit Religions:

Shamanism

Shamanism:www.merriam-webster.com/dictionary/shamanism

Definition - a religion practiced by indigenous peoples of far northern Europe and Siberia characterized by belief in an unseen world of gods, demons, and ancestral spirits responsive only to the shamans; also: any similar religion.

Usually accompanied with belief of spirit travel or spirit connection by the priest/Shaman

Similar to some American Indian Medicine Men

For healing, guidance, control, etc

Not to say all worship by American Indians was to a false God. Some may have worshipped the real Almighty God, Creator of the Universe, just as indigenous people did before Abraham. At least one American Indian tribe knew and practiced the Hebrew secret priestly prayers and songs.

Ancestor Worship

Common in Far East: contact departed ancestor's spirits

Repentance Prayer is necessary.

Father God, in Jesus name I ask You to forgive me for any involvement in any Shamanism.

I ask You to forgive me for any involvement in any worship of/from American Indians, if it was ungodly.

I ask You to forgive me for any involvement in any ancestor worship, and for any consulting them for any reason.

I repent of this and will do my best to submit to you, and to be more Christ-like and to follow You in obedience and humility, and to represent You and Jesus as best I can.

In the name of Jesus Christ, we bind every demonic spirit in my life involving any of these things. In Jesus name, we take authority over these spirits and command them to come out and leave us and our families now, and never return, and no replacements to come back in their stead. In Jesus name.

Roman Catholicism and Eastern Orthodoxy

Believe in God, Jesus, and Holy Spirit,

Great many Christians in this church

But,

People taught to pray to departed "saints"/spirits,

    Especially to Mary

    "Patron saints" assigned for people and/or special purposes/protection/guardian: (e.g.: travel, occupation, etc.)

    People do special rituals to get attention/favors of departed spirits: mass, rosary, pray to statues, way of the cross/stations, offerings, light candles, go to shrines …

    Pray to magical apparitions

    Ask a man (priest) to forgive their sins, rather than asking Jesus to forgive them.

1 Tim 2:5-6 **For there is one God and one Mediator between God and men, the Man Christ Jesus**, *6 who gave Himself a ransom for all, to be testified in due time,*

Repentance Prayer is necessary.

Father God, in Jesus name I ask You to forgive me for any involvement in any of the ungodly practices of the Roman Catholic or Eastern Orthodox Religions. I repent of praying to or communicating with statues, images, candles, shrines, apparitions, departed people, including but not limited to Mary, Joseph, Peter, Paul, St. George, St. Christopher, Popes. I only want to worship and communicate with God the Father, Jesus, and the Holy Spirit.

If I have asked a priest to forgive me of my sins, I now repent of that and I now ask Jesus to forgive me of all those sins, and forgive me of all the sins of my entire life, and to come and live in me in a greater measure than ever before.

 I repent of these things and will do my best to follow You and to represent You and Jesus as best I can.

In the name of Jesus Christ, we bind every demonic spirit in my life involving any of these things. In Jesus name, we take authority over these spirits and command them to come out and leave us and our families now, and never return, and no replacements to come back in their stead. In Jesus name.

Masons

Secret society-by invitation only

Members pledge allegiance and secrecy

Progressive revelation/indoctrination:

Secret words, phrases, pledges, rituals, vows

Per Wikipedia: In the course of three degrees, new masons will promise to keep the secrets of their degree from lower degrees and outsiders, and to support a fellow Mason in distress (as far as practicality and the law permit)

The bulk of Masonic ritual consists of degree ceremonies. Candidates for Freemasonry are progressively *initiated* into Freemasonry, first in the degree of Entered Apprentice. Some time later, in a separate ceremony, they will be *passed* to the degree of Fellowcraft, and finally they will be *raised* to the degree of Master Mason. In all of these ceremonies, the candidate is first obligated, then entrusted with passwords, signs and grips (secret handshakes) peculiar to his new rank.

The Ancient and Accepted Scottish Rite is a system of **33 degrees** (including the three Blue Lodge degrees) administered by a local or national Supreme Council. This system is popular in North America, South America and in Continental Europe. In America, the York Rite, with a similar range, administers three orders of Masonry, namely the Royal Arch, Cryptic Masonry, and Knights Templar.

Even other religions consider Masons as a religion

https://www.catholiceducation.org/en/culture/catholic-contributions/what-are-the-masons.html :

> The Catholic Church has difficulty with freemasonry because it is indeed a kind of religion unto itself. The practice of freemasonry includes temples, altars, a moral code, worship services, vestments, feast days, a hierarchy of leadership, initiation and burial rites, and promises of eternal reward and punishment. While in America, most Masons are Christian and will display a Bible on their "altar," in the same lodges or elsewhere, Jews, Muslims, Hindus or other non-Christian religions can be admitted and may use their own sacred Scriptures.

Masons, from Choosing the Truth Ministries: http://ctmin.org/christian-lucifer.php

> To understand the relationship existing between Lucifer and Freemasonry we seek out Masonic authorities to see what they have to say. Manly P. Hall, 33E Mason, referred to as one of Freemasonry's greatest philosophers,

> Book: Lost Keys of Freemasonry, pg 65: "The true Mason is not creed-bound. He realizes with the divine illumination of his lodge that as a Mason his religion must be universal: Christ, Buddha or Mohammed, the name means little, for he recognizes only the light and not the bearer. He worships at every shrine, bows before every altar, whether in temple, mosque or cathedral, realizing with his truer understanding the oneness of all spiritual truth."

And:

Book: <u>Lost Keys of Freemasonry</u>, pg 48: "When the Mason learns that the key to the warrior on the block is the proper application of the dynamo of living power, he has learned the mystery of his Craft. The seething energies of Lucifer are in his hands and before he may step onward and upward, he must prove his ability to properly apply energy."

And:

As a secret society it deliberately conceals the truth not only to outsiders but to those in the lower degrees and other members outside of the leadership. Albert Pike, 33E Mason, father of the modern Scottish Rite, is so revered that his mortal remains are buried in the walls of the Masonic Temple in Washington, DC through an act of Congress.

And:

Albert Pike states on page 321 of, Morals and Dogma;

Lucifer, the Light-bearer! Strange and mysterious name to give to the Spirit of Darkness! Lucifer, the Son of the Morning! Is it he who bears the Light, and with its splendors intolerable blinds feeble, sensual, or selfish Souls? Doubt it not!

And:

On page 162 of, Encyclopedia of Freemasonry by Dr. Albert Mackey, 33E Mason, we are told;

"Freemasonry is not Christianity, nor a substitute for it. It does not meddle with sectarian creeds or doctrines, but teaches fundamental religious truth."

Repentance Prayer is necessary.

In the name of Jesus Christ, I hereby reject and renounce any involvement in, or association with, or any heritage of, the Masonic religion and any of its affiliates. I reject everything about it, and cut it off from my and my family, in the name of Jesus Christ.

Father God, in Jesus name I ask You to forgive me for any involvement in any of various branches of the Masonic religion. I repent of praying to or communicating with any of their deities, the great architect of the universe, and to any of their historical or mythical personalities. I repent of taking any secret vows. I repent of invoking or agreeing with any curses, upon myself, my family, my posterity, or others. I repent of these things and will do my best to follow You and to represent You and Jesus as best I can. Lead me into all truth. Thank you, Father.

In the name of Jesus Christ, we bind every demonic spirit in my life involving any of these things. In Jesus name, we take authority over these spirits and command them to come out and leave us and our families now, and never return, and no replacements to come back in their stead. In Jesus name.

Thomas and Fay Velez

Chapter 6: Dominating Spirits

Dominating Spirits want to dominate you

*1 Peter 5:8 **[Be sober], [be vigilant];** because your adversary the devil, as a roaring lion, walketh about, **seeking whom he may devour**:*

Devil is looking for your vulnerability

Devil knows **your attitude affects your vulnerability**, which affects your

- Attitude, Choices, Behavior

Wants to make you lose control of:

1. Your emotions

2. Your thoughts/rationality

3. Your sensing/recognizing Holy Spirit

4. -Your control of your body

Lose Control of Emotions:

<u>**UNFORGIVENESS**</u>:

Binds your emotions

Must forgive, to free ourselves

Does not mean we have to let people do it again

Take a minute to repent of any unforgiveness.

<u>**ANGER, HATRED**</u>:

Entices quick response to hurt/get even

Doesn't forget, keeps emotion/pain/adrenaline high

Take a minute to repent of any unforgiveness.

<u>**FEAR:**</u>

Many times, from a trauma

Situations were out-of-control

Causes panic, inability to perceive or respond correctly or at all (e.g.: paralysis or over-reacting)

Prayer/Command:

In the name of Jesus Christ, we bind every demonic spirit that would try to make us lose control of our emotions, including all spirits of fear, paralysis, panic, claustrophobia, and choking. In Jesus name, we bind these and any other spirits that have gained entry into any of these people's lives through any kind of trauma.

In Jesus name, we take authority over these spirits and command them to come out and leave us and our families now, and never return, and no replacements to come back in their stead. In Jesus name.

Lose Control of Thoughts/Rationality:

SPIRITS OF CONFUSION:

MIND-BINDING:

Unable to focus clearly on things, especially ways of escaping circumstances.

Person feels like in a "cloud"

ANGER/HATRED:

Entices quick response to hurt/get even

Does not forget, keeps emotion/pain/adrenaline high

LYING/DECEIT:

Hides the truth

To cause wrong rationale, understanding, decisions, emotions, actions

LEVIATHAN:

Twists the incoming words so hearer does not correctly understand speaker (hears or suspects the worst)

Many times, perceived as an insult, etc.

Many times, hidden or thought to be a simple misunderstanding

Many times, built upon a foundation of rejection, insecurity, pride, lack of/or violated trust or emotional trauma

Many times because of ancestor's participation in occult, Masons, etc.

Spirits of Confusion (Prayer/Command)

In the name of Jesus Christ, we bind every demonic spirit that would try to make us lose control of our thoughts and rationality. We bind every mind-binding spirit, every spirit causing a loss of the ability to focus, every spirit causing a cloud or haze over our thinking. In Jesus name, we bind every spirit of anger and hatred. In Jesus name, we bind every lying and deceitful spirit operating in our lives. In Jesus name, we bind every Leviathan spirit, and every other spirit that would try to cause us confusion or cause us to hear or perceive or understand things incorrectly. In Jesus name, we bind any other spirits trying to cause miscommunications with, to, or from us.

In Jesus' name, we cast these evil spirits out, and command them never to return, and no more to come back in their stead, in Jesus name.

<u>JEZEBEL SPIRIT:</u>

Not male or female

Wants to CONTROL

- <u>First Method: Be in control, and recognized as such</u>

- <u>Alternative Method: Control the one who is in control</u>

- <u>If unable to control: DESTROY</u>

    o Destroy person in control

    o Destroy the entire work/ministry

        ▪ Slander, lies, seduction, false accusations, discord, corruption, whatever it takes—vicious

Desperately wants to stop Holy Spirit

- E.g.: Holy Spirit flow, gifts, spontaneity, prophecy, salvations, etc.

Always wants to keep decisionmaker off guard

- Surprises

- Manipulation

- Gossip, Backbiting

- Relentless

- Will not take no for an answer

- Will demand a reason for your refusal

- Will continue to argue

- Will change the subject, rather than agree

- You MUST SAY NO, again and again

- You DO NOT owe them a reason

Jezebel Spirit (Prayer/Command)

Father God, we ask You to help us recognize the spirit of Jezebel operating through people. We ask You to show us how to counter each of their attacks against us. Help us to not be surprised, and to thwart their every move. Help us to remain swift to hear you, and to spontaneously and immediately hear and obey you, to march forward victoriously in every area of our lives.

In the name of Jesus Christ, we bind every Jezebel spirit operating against us. In Jesus, name, we bind every other evil spirit that would try to hinder us in our walk with God or come against what God has given us or has for us.

In Jesus' name, we cast these evil spirits out, and command them never to return, and no more to come back in their stead, in Jesus name.

Lose Control of Sensing/Recognizing Holy Spirit:

<u>SPIRIT OF REBELLION/WITCHCRAFT:</u>

Much like Jezebel spirit, but different motivations

Choosing rebellion/witchcraft **is a CHOICE**, not a confusion or deception while trying to follow God.

Wants POWER

Will go for the power

- Willing to hurt others to get power

- Many times wants power OVER others

- Built upon power, fear and selfishness, not love or unity

Will chase the supernatural, wherever it comes from

The higher one goes, the more at risk they are

Enticement, deceptions, entrapment is progressive

Witchcraft/Rebellion: Repentance Prayer is necessary.

Father God and Jesus, I ask You to forgive me for choosing to rebel against You and choose witchcraft. Forgive me for choosing to seek power rather than to seek You. Forgive me for being willing to hurt others and to try to exert control over them. I repent any involvement in any form of witchcraft and the occult in any form. I repent of this and will do my best to submit to you, and to be more Christ-like and to follow You in obedience and humility, and to represent You and Jesus as best I can.

In Jesus name, I renounce and reject any inheritance of witchcraft or the occult and cut off any such words or actions of my ancestors if any such thing occurred.

In the name of Jesus Christ, we bind every demonic spirit in my life involving any of these things. In Jesus name, we take authority over these spirits and command them to come out and leave us and our families now, and never return, and no replacements to come back in their stead. In Jesus name.

FAMILIAR SPIRITS:

Want you to follow/seek them for guidance, companionship,

May imitate God, Jesus, Holy Spirit

May imitate Angels, Saints, ancestors, deceased persons

Can be generational, assigned by/at/through birth or as a child by/from/through adults

Can be "picked-up" through occult inspired or dedicated objects, songs, movies, TV, people (e.g.: carriers) readings, games, etc.

Familiar Spirits: Repentance Prayer is necessary

In Jesus name, I renounce and reject any relationships with any familiar spirits. I only accept the relationship of God's Spirit and only that which is truly from Him, and I will follow no other. I will not worship any other Spirit, other than the Spirit of the Living God.

In Jesus name, I bind every familiar spirit and spirit of deception, and command you to get out of my life and be gone forever, and no more to come back.

SPIRITS OF FALSE RELIGIONS:

Different than Religious Spirits

Much like familiar spirits

Want you to follow/seek them for guidance, comfort, etc

Imitate God, Jesus, Holy Spirit, false gods, spirit guides (e.g.: animals, demons, etc.)

Can be generational, assigned at/by/through birth or as a child by adults,

Want your worship/adoration, even obedience

Spirit of False Religions: Repentance Prayer is necessary

In Jesus name, I renounce and reject all religious spirits operating in my life. I renounce all these evil spirits of deception, and I will not follow you or worship you or seek you for any reason from henceforth.

I bind you all in the name, the power, the authority, and the blood of Jesus Christ and cast you out of my live forever.

SPIRITS OF PERVERSION:

Homosexual, child abuse, LGBT, "meanness", many others

*Lev 20:13 (Amp V) If a man lies with a male as if he were a woman, both men have committed an offense (something **perverse**, unnatural, abhorrent, and detestable); they shall surely be put to death; their blood shall be upon them.*

*Rom 1:28-31 And even as they did not like to retain God in their knowledge, **God gave them over to a debased mind**, to do those things which are not fitting; being filled with all unrighteousness, sexual immorality, wickedness, covetousness, maliciousness; full of envy, murder, strife, deceit, evil-mindedness; they are whisperers, backbiters, haters of God, violent, proud, boasters, inventors of evil things, disobedient to parents, undiscerning, untrustworthy, unloving, unforgiving, unmerciful;*

Lu 17:2 It were better for him that a millstone were hanged about his neck, and he cast into the sea, than that he should offend (entice to sin) one of these little ones.

Spirit of Perversion: Repentance Prayer is necessary

Father God help me to think clearly and understand your will clearly. I repent of any and all perverse mindsets and actions that I might have accumulated in my life. I accept your will and way as described in your Word, the Holy Bible. I reject the normalcy of homosexuality, abortions, meanness, debauchery, unnecessary violence, slavery, vileness, and abuse of others.

In Jesus name, I renounce and reject all spirits and mindsets of perversion operating in my life.

I bind you all in the name, the power, the authority, and the blood of Jesus Christ and cast you out of my live forever.

RELIGIOUS SPIRITS:

Self-righteous

Critical/judgmental of others

Works dominated, not mercy or grace dominated

Always negative of others/quick to condemn

See themselves as better than others

PRIDEFUL

Willing to gossip

- Will call gossip as prayer

This spirit blinds people to others efforts/worth

People unable to see themselves as having this spirit

Religious Spirit: Repentance Prayer is necessary.

Father God and Jesus, I ask You to help me recognize any self-righteous attitude in me. I ask You to forgive me for choosing to be self-righteous, and for putting myself above others, as being more important or more self-righteous than them. I ask You to forgive me for being critical and judgmental of others. Forgive me for being negative of others, and even putting them down verbally. Forgive me of gossiping about others. Help me to see the value of others, and to be merciful to them, and an extension of your love towards them.

In the name of Jesus Christ, we bind every demonic spirit in my life involving any of these things. In Jesus name, we take authority over these spirits and command them to come out and, and never return, in Jesus name.

I repent of this and will do my best to submit to you, and to be more Christ-like and to follow You in obedience and humility, and to represent You and Jesus as best I can.

Lose Control of Your Body

PYTHON:

A suffocating/constricting/tiring spirit

Resists expansion/freedom

People feel squeezed, restricted

When people resist, there is a holding/balance

When people rest, the Python spirit constricts tighter, allowing less freedom or rest

Objective: to wear you out

- To squeeze out joy, life, excitement, hope
- Take away your freedom
- To give up the will to fight/resist
- To give up the will to live

Weights:

Not really a spirit, but a tool of the demonic spirits

Like weights placed on your shoulders or chest: you feel a burden

Intended to weigh you down, like putting rocks into the backpack of a hiker/climber

Just recognize it, and cast it off with the name of Jesus

- You will actually feel them lift off and feel lighter

Commanding: Crushing Spirits/devices: Python and Weights

In the name of Jesus Christ, we bind every python spirit and command them to let go now, and come out now, and, and never return, in Jesus name.

In the name of Jesus Christ, we cast off every demonic weight and every burden put on us by the enemy, and we cast it all off now, in Jesus name.

SPIRITS OF INFIRMITY:

Disabling-to restrict body's capability to be used for God

- To combat faith in God, healing, promises, prayer, etc.

- Disguises as natural physical/physiological/biological/chemical problems

Hinders natural healing, &/or immune system

Can be generational curse

Can be curses issued by ancestors: e.g.: Masons, etc.

Can come from agreements with demonic powers, demonic healings, demonic gifts, etc. (price to be paid)

Commanding: Spirits of Infirmity

In the name of Jesus Christ, we bind every spirit of infirmity and command them to let go now, and come out now, and, and never return, in Jesus name. In Jesus name we command healing to take place in our physical bodies.

Most times, it seems to help greatly if you pray for healing also. Usually, it is good to have a person make sure they have no unforgiveness in their heart first.

More about this in the book/section "Personal Spiritual Warfare".

SPIRITS OF ADDICTION:

Using the mechanisms of your body against yourself

Prevention the best medicine

Don't start, don't program your body to want it

Intends to disable your control, and take control

Can be generational curse

Can be demonic addiction as well as physical/chemical

> Can be linked and symbiotic

Much written about addictions

DEMONIC ADDICTIONS:

Demons have personalities: they act out THEIR lusts, etc. through a person

Demons want to destroy God's creations, especially His people. They want to hurt God the only way they can.

Demons want to derail/stop God's plan for people.

Demons want to show God that people want them more than they want God.

Commanding: Addictions

Father God take away the desire of the addictions afflicting me. Give me the strength and joy to overcome this addiction. Help me to see things clearly. Help me to forget the pleasures of the addiction and remember the pain and cost of it. Help my body and mind not to need it.

In the name of Jesus Christ, we bind every spirit of addiction and command them to let go now, and come out now, and, and never return, in Jesus name. In Jesus name we command healing to take place in our physical bodies.

Many times, it seems to help greatly if you pray for healing also. Usually, it is good to have a person make sure they have no unforgiveness in their heart first.

More about this in the book/section "Personal Spiritual Warfare".

SPIRITS OF SICKNESS/DISEASES

NOT ALL sicknesses/diseases are demonic

Most probably not

We live in a fallen world, in fragile human bodies

History shows we will all wear out and die, if we don't die first, until the end- however that works out

Use all means at your disposal to get healed:

-Prayers, declarations, quoting scriptures and promises, doctors, medicine

Except: occultic, demonic, ungodly means

It is not either / or:

- Do them all

- Don't give up

- Speak in faith, don't let your words cancel your prayers/faith

Get others to pray with you

Do personal spiritual warfare

64

Expect results!

Give the Lord a body to use that is physically fit

Chapter 7: Prayers

Importance of prayer:

What is prayer? It is just talking to the Lord.

Prayer builds character in us and it transforms us into the image of God.

Prayer should not be a one-way conversation, but a two-way conversation, allowing the Lord to speak too.

The Lord's Prayer is an amazing example of how we should pray

Matthew 6:9-13 Our Father who is in heaven, Hallowed be Your name 'Your kingdom come, Your will be done On earth as it is in heaven. 'Give us this day our daily bread. 'And forgive us our debts, as we have forgiven our debtors. And do not lead us into temptation, but deliver us from evil. [For Yours is the kingdom and the power and the glory forever. Amen.]'

This prayer gives us the ingredients we need, and it teaches us how we should pray.

As we pray it opens our heart to God.

Prayer allows God to mold and to make us into the person we need to become.

God is our spiritual and physical healer, and as we continue to spend time with him, He will build a relationship with us, and we will experience life transforming, life renewing, and intimacy with Him.

James 5:16 The fervent prayer of a righteous man accomplishes much.

Prayer breaks down barriers in our life and brings clarity to us.

Hebrews 4:16 Therefore let us approach the throne of grace with confidence and without fear, so that we may receive mercy and find grace to help in time of need.

Prayer is a weapon we can use against the demonic.

There are different ways to pray:

Pray the word of God

Example: Lord, according to your word in 2 Timothy 1:7, I thank you that you did not give me a spirit of fear, but of power and love and a sound mind in Jesus name.

Decrees

Decreeing is, taking God's words and what God has for us, and saying it out loud with authority, and seeing things change in our life and others lives.

Example:

In the name of Jesus, I decree my children will be saved, filled with the Holy Spirit, and will walk for Jesus all the days of their lives.

In the name of Jesus, I decree my house will be paid in full within one year.

In the name of Jesus, I decree door's for ministry will open up for me.

Claiming your prophetic words over yourself

Speak the prophetic words that have been spoken over you by prophets, or that the Lord Himself has told you.

Example: Lord, in the name of Jesus I claim the prophetic word that was spoken over me regarding me being debt free to come to pass in my life in Jesus name.

Praying in tongues

Tongues is not a human language, it is a heavenly language, and when we pray in tongues, it unlocks doors to our spirit life and manifestations of the Holy Spirit. This is because the words are spoken from the Holy Spirit, and are definitely in accordance with the will of God.

Tongues is our helper, our comforter, our intercessor, our secret weapon, and our faithful friend.

Praying in tongues builds us up, and it has powerful benefits to our spiritual life.

Prayers to receive more from the Lord:

Prayer for more boldness & confidence:

Lord, I ask You to give me more confidence to lay my hands on the sick, believing them to recover. Lord let Your healing power flow through me and go into sick people and heal them, attacking the enemy's work until they are fully restored back to health again. In Your Word, it is stated that when believers lay hands on the sick, they would be made well again. Today I make the decision to pray for the sick so Your healing power can be administered to others through me in Jesus' name!

Lord I believe and trust that Your power will be released into sick people when I lay my hands on them. Just like medicine that slowly works to heal a medical condition, the power of God that flows from the Holy Spirit in me when I lay my hands-on sick people will cause them to be progressively restored to health and well-being. Healing the sick is a part of my responsibility and inheritance in You, so I confess that when I lay my hands on sick people just as You did, they will be healed. Amen

Prayer for more desire to worship:

Lord, I ask You to give me a greater desire to worship You. Lord, help me know and understand the blessings and breakthroughs I will receive as I worship You, in Jesus name. Lord, start a fire of passion for you inside of me. Help me burst out in praise, worship and thanksgiving to You, in Jesus name. Thank You Lord, that your word tells me that a merry heart does good like a medicine, so Lord, as I step out each day and sing and worship and praise You, I ask You to help me feel your tangible touch, let your presence consume me, and that I would walk in your intimacy and glory daily, in Jesus name. Amen

Prayer for more Joy:

Lord, I ask You to help me walk in a greater level of joy, Your joy Lord, the joy of the Lord. Lord, help me to recognize and be thankful for the things in my life that bring me joy. Lord, help me increase that joy by getting more sensitive to You and those around me. Help me to grow in faith and be more joyful. Lord, help me to have that peace and joy that only your Spirit can bring. Lord help me to share that joy with others. Amen

Prayer for more faith to be healed:

Father, in the Name of Jesus, I confess Your Word concerning health and healing over myself. Lord, the Bible says that what You have said, will not return to you void, but it will accomplish what it says. In the name of Jesus, I believe that I am healed according to 1 Peter 2:24. Your Word says that Jesus Himself took my infirmities and bore my sicknesses and infirmities on the cross with Him, so that I would not have to be under them anymore. Lord, I believe and stand on Your Word and agree and declare that You paid for my healing, and I am healed and will see it in my body, here on Earth.

Satan, I speak to you in Jesus' Name and I proclaim that your principalities, powers, rulers of the darkness of this world, and spiritual wickedness in heavenly places are bound from operating against me in any way, in Jesus name.

I am loosed from your assignment. I am the property of God and I give you no place to operate in me. I dwell in the secret place of the Most High God and I abide under the shadow of the Almighty, whose power no enemy can withstand, in Jesus name.

Now, Father, I believe Your Word which says the angel of the Lord camps round about me and delivers me from every evil work. No evil shall befall me, no plague or calamity shall come near my dwelling. I confess that the Word of God is in me and it is life and medicine to-my flesh. The Holy Spirit operates in me and I am led by the Holy Spirit, making me free from the law of sin and death. Lord I thank You and give You praise and glory that health and healing are mine now, and that I will walk in a greater level of faith and healing than ever before in Jesus' Name. Amen

Chapter 8: Deliverance: Personal and Team; Activation and Practice

Details for Personal Deliverance are contained in the Personal Spiritual Warfare material referenced in this book.

Why Team Ministry? 3 Reasons

1-Multiple People receiving: more accurate, more breadth

- We minister by the Holy Spirit, & different people have different giftings & strengths
    - Discerning of Spirits
    - Prophecy
    - Words of Knowledge
    - Tongues: keep volume low to not distract & so people can hear

2-Only one ministers at a time. When not ministering, others listen to Holy Spirit.

3-Safety in numbers

- Physical, spiritual, verbal
- Witnesses: accusations, etc.

How:

- Introduction; Be friendly, calm, pleasant, polite, respectful
- Team leader start, standing directly in-front-of the client
    - Others stand quietly beside or behind, not distracting or interrupting
- Take turns:

- When team leader finishes, they move back & to side, and next minister steps up front
- Process of ministering and rotation repeats until ministers have nothing more to say
  - Usually each minister looks at each other to see who has something & is ready
- When done, leader or designate closes, & someone gives declaration sheet & explains

<u>Why this way:</u>

- Unity is very important for the Holy Spirit to move
- Politeness & calmness are important for client confidence & cooperation
  - Not threatened, don't become agitated or vengeful, etc.
- Every minister can contribute; Holy Spirit can use every minister

The client should leave glad that they came, feel like a load was lifted and even joyful, and if applicable that healing possibly took place, etc. In other words, their faith was lifted up and they were glad they did it, and would recommend this to friends and others, rather than being fearful, angry or speaking against this ministry, this kind of ministry or CI.

Chapter 9: Personal Spiritual Warfare

Because of the voluminous amount of material, the Personal Spiritual Warfare material is contained in a separate book by Thomas Velez, titled:

Personal Spiritual Warfare

The "How To Do It" Book"

A paper copy of this book is available from the author in person.

A paper copy or an electronic (Kindle) version are both available on Amazon.com.

Notes:

Chapter 10: Healing

Healing:

Hebrew 13:8 Jesus Christ is the same yesterday, today and forever.

The same healing power that touched lives 2000 years ago is still available to touch us today. The same power that touched the man with leprosy, and the woman with the issue of blood, and the lame man He will do for us.

Isaiah 53:4-5 But He was wounded for our transgressions, He was crushed for our wickedness [our sin, our injustice, our wrongdoing];The punishment [required] for our well-being fell on Him, and by His stripes we are healed.

Jesus does not change, He is the same yesterday, today and forever, (Hebrew13:8)

Acts 10:38 "God anointed Jesus of Nazareth with the Holy Ghost and power: who went about doing good and healing all that were oppressed of the devil, for God was with him.

So why are Christians still sick?

Because we are living in a fallen world, where physical death, and sickness still exist, because of sin and it affects everyone, it will be present here on earth until Jesus returns.

But God still heals, and we have to stand and fight for our healing.

We have to believe that all things are possible with God.

Jesus does not change.

Satan wants to keep us sick and bound, so we have to war and fight for our healing and to keep our healing even though Jesus has already paid for it.

Col. 2:14 Having canceled the charge of our legal indebtedness, which stood against us and condemned us; he has taken it away, nailing it to the cross.

We have to cancel all of Satan's legal claims he has on us, such as generational curses, or negative words written or spoken.

Mark 3:27 in fact, no one can enter a strong man's house without first tying him up. Then he can plunder the strong man's house.

God has given us the authority over sickness. We just have to believe.

Mark 16:17-18 tells us: And these signs will follow those who believe: In My name they will cast out demons; they will speak with new tongues; they will take up serpents; and if they drink anything deadly, it will by no means hurt them; they will lay hands on the sick, and they will recover." They will pick up snake with their hands; and when they drink deadly poison, it will not hurt them at all; they will place their hands on the sick people, and they will get well.

The Holy Spirit is with us to impart His power when we pray in Jesus name for someone to be healed, as we step out and lay hands on the sick, God will work with us to bring healing to those in need.

God's word is powerful to decree and declare over ourselves when we or someone else is sick.

Ex. 15:26: I am the Lord that healeth thee

Ex. 23:25-26: I will take sickness away from the midst of you, and the number of your days I will fulfill.

Deut. 23:5: I turned the curse into a blessing to you, because I Love you.

Psalms 91:10: no plaque shall come near your   dwelling.

Psalms 103:3: I healed all your diseases

Psalms 107:20: I sent my word and healed you
and delivered you from destruction.

Matthew 8:17: I took your infirmities and I bore your sickness.

Matthew 15:26: healing is the children's bread.

1Peter 2:24: by my stripes you were healed.

God has many ways He uses to heal us, and so many times our ignorance and unbelief blocks God's healing power from flowing to us and through us.

Our personal sin can keep us from being healed.

We live in a world of sin, and this world is full of germs, viruses, and diseases, and we get sick, just because of the environment we live in.

Satan is another reason we don't get healed.

Ways the Lord heals:

1. In the natural

2. The nutritional way

3. Through science

4. Medical arts

5. His divine supernatural healing

Difference between miracles and healings

Miracles happen in an instant.

They are instantaneous and complete healing
that goes beyond any law of science and beyond any human ability.

Miracles are defined in the Bible, as an effect or extraordinary event in the physical world that surpasses all known human or natural powers
and is ascribed to a supernatural cause.

Miracles are a work of God!

Healing is a process.

Which means that the individual becomes completely whole over a longer time period.

Every healing, whether it is a miracle or a process, we still have to make the right chose daily, and continue to war and fight to keep our healing.

Tools to help you walk in miracles and healing:

1. release the power of God's kingdom from within you
2. pray in the Holy Ghost to build your faith
3. cancel all legal claims and curses of evil spirits over yourself.
4. bind and uproot the strongman of disease and affliction
5. speak healing and restoration by the blood of Jesus
6. put faith with action and give God the glory

Keys to help you unlock your healing:

1. Meditate on the Lord
2. Clothe yourselves in Bible humility
3. Walk in love toward God and others
4. Walk free of offense
5. Take authority over our words that we let come out of our mouth.
    *   Do not cancel your healing by denying it

Biblical reasons why someone may not get healed:

1. Unconfessed sin
2. Lack of faith
3. Not asking God to heal you

   "James 4:2 we have not because we ask not."

4. You need deliverance
5. A higher purpose
6. God's glory
7. God's time

Natural reason why you may not get healed:

6. Doubting
7. Unforgiveness in your heart
8. We don't ask God to heal us
9. You may need a deliverance

Reasons we maybe the reason we are not healed:

1. Not getting enough rest or sleep
2. Not eating the right kinds of food
3. Not exercising
4. Stress

Prescriptions from the Lord for us to walk in divine health:

1. His word

2. Rejoice and to be happy

3. Do not worry

Practical guidelines we need to do when we pray for others:

1. Do not touch an open wound.

2. Wash your hands after you pray for someone with an open wound.

3. Be respectable to who you are ministering to

4. Never pray behind closed doors to the opposite sex by yourself

5. Do not minister to a child alone

When people are sick, we need to get to the root cause of the sickness:

Such as: Unforgiveness, word curses, generational curses, or negative soul ties.

So, before you pray for someone, talk to them, and find out the details regarding their illness.

Healing was the foundation of Jesus ministry, and most of Jesus work on earth had to do with healing.

Healing is a process, and our freedom has to be walked out one step at a time.

It is like peeling an onion, one layer at a time.

But the key is to keep going forward and never looking back, and seeing yourself as a victor, not a victim.

Tools we can use to receive healing:

Praise and worship

It unlocks doors and breaks chains and brings healing to us.

It is the key which we can use to unlock doors, tear down strongholds and purchase our breakthrough.

It brings healing to our physical body, mind and spirit.

It makes the enemy flee

It invites the presence of the Lord into our situation.

Worship paves the way for God's power to make miracles happen.

Praying in tongues:

It is a hotline to God, the devil cannot understand tongues, so he cannot interfere with what you are praying.

When you pray in tongues you are praying exactly what needs to be prayed.

When we pray in tongues the angels listen and they look at the Lord, and when they get the ok, they go out and implement what we are praying in tongues.

Tongues is an amazing tool to have when you are sick and don't know what is wrong with you.

God's Word: "The Bible"

Pray healing scriptures over yourself

Quote healing declarations

Write down things you need healing for and declare them daily until you see the healing manifested.

Listen to healing scriptures

Joy:

Neh. 8:10 tells us the joy of the Lord is our strength.

This kind of joy comes from the Lord, and it transforms and regenerates us.

This joy brings healing and happiness to us

The healing power of joy will bring a change in us, if we allow it to.

Joy brings healing to our bodies

Joy and laughter support both our physical and emotional health.

Joy is priceless medicine, it is fun, free and easy to use.

God's joy supply is limitless

Singing:

The internet tells us, singing promotes health because it increases the circulation, and a good circulation is a sign of good health.

Keep your healing:

1. Don't accept Satan's lies
2. Resist the devil and he will flee
3. Don't doubt
4. Go to war against the devil
5. And allow a great expectation of what God will do for you to arise in your heart
6. And receive your healing,
7. Recognize it
8. Accept it
9. And hang onto it
10. Not negative words.

Chapter 11: Healing, Medical Explanations

Many of the pains and infirmities people experience in their lifetime are due to misalignment of their bones, especially their backbone, and from pinched nerves resulting from that. Alignment of the bones many times instantly relieves the pressure on a nerve, causing the related pain to go away instantly.

I am first going to explain the basic biology of our skeletal structure. Feel free to take notes in the space provided.

Then, I will explain how to pray and see instantaneous miracles involving this, right before your eyes, in this class. You will see legs and arms "grow out" by portions of their back being adjusted, and other things involving the skeletal structure. All this is done by using the name of Jesus Christ, not by any physical adjusting of any part of the body.

These healing techniques were learned from a healing ministry team: Charles and Frances Hunter. We took their classes, were on their healing teams, and taught their classes to others. They have two very good, highly recommended books, listed below, as well as many other good books and teaching videos.

Their books are:

How to Heal the Sick, by Charles and Frances Hunter, Kingwood, TX, Hunter Books, c1981

Handbook for Healing, by Charles and Frances Hunter, Kingwood, TX, Hunter Books, c1987

Notes:

Chapter 12: Healing Demonstrations, Activation, Exercises

Notes:

Contact Information

Contact us through the contact form on our website:

ThomasVelez.com

To order more books by Thomas and Fay Velez:

- Get Free, Stay Free

To order more books by Thomas Velez:

- Personal Spiritual Warfare
- Army of the Lord Arising
- Understanding the Book of Revelation
- Antichrist Invades Earth
- God Saved My Life 29 Times

Order online from websites:

ThomasVelez.com

and at:

Amazon.com